FROM TREE

TO TREE

I0447217

BIRDS FLY
&
THE TREE OF LIFE

ARTWORK AND STORIES
BY
SHERRI LOUISE JONES

THE REALITY OF
EVERY DAY IS A MIRACLE

A long time ago I started writing stories about some of the things that I have noticed or came upon. I call it (The Reality of Every Day is a Miracle). This book has some of the short stories from that book. It also has some short stories from my book (Birds Big and Small). If we look at all of the things that go on in one day, we can find many blessings.

THE COMMUNICATION TREE COPYRIGHT © 2012
ARTWORK AND STORIES BY SHERRI LOUISE JONES

FROM

TREE

TO

TREE

BIRDS FLY
&
THE TREE OF LIFE

FROM TREE TO TREE

Many birds like to build there homes in trees, they build nest using twigs, grasses and fibers. The nests are thick, very well made and sturdy. They are very well weaved baskets and bowls. Many birds like to fly from tree to tree, they use the branches to perch on while looking around or resting from flying.

Children need to be taught about the tree of life and that the trees grow from the earth. Thees grow and expand they are alive, they have roots and so do we, they are individual. Trees are male and female they can plant seeds for baby trees. Trees have ancestors and roots. They have life cycles, many change colors and leaves according to the seasons and atmospheres. All trees have purposes on this earth. They are medicines and grow food for many different kinds of animals, birds, insects and human beings. They provide shelter and homes for many forms of life. They serve many purposes.

Some people use leafs, bark, branches, needles and roots to make teas. Some use pine needles for a cleansing and shampoo. On a hot day many different kind of trees are nice for shade, many of the leafs shaded from the sun are cool, they are very nice to feel and hold.

Cedar branches are my favorite. Cedar is considered very holy to many Native tribes. It is used for many spiritual cleaning purposes internal and external. It is used by

many as a form of protection from evil and can be made into a tea for use as a blood purifier, to rid toxins in the blood. The bitter taste can make the mouth water causing saliva. An individuals own saliva is a natural medicine.

The sap inside of a maple tree can be turned into maple syrup and maple sugar. A hole is tapped into the tree and the clear fluid comes out. It is cooked until it becomes a nice thick brown syrup. This is a natural form of sugar. Natural sugars are much healthier then bad chemically processed sugars.

Much of our furniture that we use and the paper that we write on are made from trees. If you look at a library or a book store you can see that it took many trees to make all of the books. If you go to a grocery or department store you can see cardboard boxes, tissues and many other items made from trees. Wooden bowls have been being made for thousands of years.

People also burn wood from trees in a fire for warmth, cooking and cleansing. Many people pray using fire, burn things for purification and submission of prayers. The smoke is acknowledged to carry the prayers to the creator within many cultures. Tobacco is used within this to offer prayers to the creator by offering the tobacco to the fire. This is the beliefs within the culture of many Native American tribes. Trees and fire are considered holy in almost every culture around the world. While burning the fragrance can be a medicine to the brain. Many have medicinal properties and are considered very holy to many different cultures. My favorites are willow, birch and cedar. This is not recommended to do if you are not familiar with these medicines. If the fires are not cared for while burning the smoke and the fire can cause very much damage to a person's lungs and body. A fire could spread and cause many things to burn. It is wise to always take care of and cherish our sacred fires.

A fire can be made naturally from tree branches, grass and brush. It is made by rubbing sticks together real fast with friction. These are the same things that many birds use to build there nest. For children it is not wise to try this without an adult present.

One of my sisters had a big weeping willow tree in her front yard. After the tree was cut down, a whole lot of birds flocked to the tree that was lying on the ground. The birds were gathering their medicine. They collect the medicine before it is gone. Salicylic Acid is a chemical in the tree that is an aspirin type of medicine. Good for aches, pains and fevers. It is one of the favorite types of food for many birds. It is also used as an aspirin by humans. Many aspirins that are sold in the stores have salicylic acid in them. Precaution warning, that type of acid is not good for all humans. It is amazing how nature works. Most birds instinctly know what to eat in order to keep themselves happy and healthy.

Every tree has a medicinal purpose for some form of life. They can be infected with diseases and die. If the earth becomes sick from toxins the trees will be destroyed as well as all life and it will affect the future of our young. It is said that all of the things that we need to heal ourselves and the earth from diseases are right here on and within the earth. If we take care of the earth we may find these cures. If we teach the children about taking care of the tree of life, we have made a better life for other generations of trees including our own ancestral trees.

A lot of elders say that all of the medicines that we need are right here on this earth. Everything we eat is a medicine, but some of it is bad medicine. So if we eat good things, it is a good medicine and if we eat bad things, it is a bad medicine. It's common sense. It is something to think and question ourselves about, how much do we love ourselves?

Many people were not taught respect for others or themselves. They may learn within time as to the fact that we are all human. This is when people learn who they are as human beings. Self truth!

We need to teach the children to care for one another and the earth. We need to teach them about humanity, kindness and gentleness within their own nature. One of the main things to learn is that we are all equal within creation, discrimination is a sin.

We all came from a seed and roots that are a mixture of our parents and their parents. They are our ancestors. No seed is the exact same. So we are individual human beings. Our ancestors may be all of the same culture or of many different cultures. We are of our parents and their ancestors. Being individual we have our own individual minds to make decisions, learn and to form beliefs.

If a person asks, "Where are your roots from?" They are usually meaning what land you were born to. They are referring to your ancestral family tree as to, where did you and your family come from? What is your ancestry and from where? In the ways of many Native American tribes if a person ask another Native person, "Who are you?" They are usually inquiring about the ancestral roots as well as name. Different cultures have different ways as to referral of this question.

Today is April 16, 2012 my birthday. Yesterday I saw butterflies, spring has sprung early this year and it was a warm day. The butterflies have started to birth from their cocoons within the trees and plants. They were caterpillars who have grown wings and now can fly. They make use of the trees for homes as well the birds and other beings. They are of the winged ones. I had also noticed that the mosquitoes are early this year too. They are also of the winged ones. Many trees have started to bud and bloom early.

Last night while taking a break from writing about trees. I went outside and started to pray by a tree that I visit frequently. I told my dog to sit next to me and said, "Creator what do this dog and I need. What do you want me to do with this book? I want to help somehow in this world and will the book do some good?" The wind started to whip and I noticed that the tree branches full of leaves were shaking real hard right at me, just a few feet in front and above. It was shaking in the direction of the east as to where I was standing. So that is where I left my prayers. The dog was not sitting anymore she was running in circles around me real fast counter clockwise. Then I thought well the dog needs to run and have fun, plus she has circled me. Then the big tree branch shook up and down. I said well I guess that must have been a yes, thank you!

I saw a big white bird fly out of that same tree last summer. I didn't know if it was an albino eagle or an albino hawk. I was out there two days ago and saw a woodpecker, robins, white dove and red cardinals, all within ten minutes of each other. I had my camera and tried to get pictures and the camera had strange issues, the birds are not close enough or fly away too soon. For some reason I have a hard time getting pictures of the birds. I was told a long time ago, if things happen spiritually then they are not to be filmed or cannot at times be filmed. Many different things happen, I wonder?

I went outside the next day after the big wind and saw that it was so powerful that it had broken branches off of many trees in the woods. I noticed that many trees had bloomed. I picked myself some flower branches for my birthday. I like the way they smell and they made the home prettier.

My granddaughter Brooklyn and I walked in the woods out here one day. She had a new camera and wanted some wildlife pictures. She was six years old. We only saw one bird and it was too far away for a picture. The only animal we saw was a small lost dog wandering around through the trees. We found it's owner and she took a picture of it. The dog smiled while she took his picture.

Another day we walked around out there without a camera. A big golden eagle flew out of a tree. She made up a song about it. A few days later I was telling a neighbor lady about it. She is almost 90 years old. She said that around that same time a big golden eagle landed in the yard that we share. It was staring at her while facing her big picture window. It opened it wings and started flapping them while looking at her through the window. She spoke about this with excitement. We had wondered if it was the same eagle and if that was where it went. Brooklyn sang the song to her.

She is one of the nicest and friendliest elder women I have ever met. Many children in the neighborhood enjoy her kindness. When she sees them, she always smiles and tells them what good kids they are. She has a way about her that just sparkles when she *speaks. I believe that the eagle was a message from the creator letting her know that she is blessed.*

I have seen many miraculous things with bald eagles. An elder told me that when I am scared and confused to pray to the eagles. He said that the eagles will guide me.

I SAW AN EAGLE

I saw an eagle flying from a tree.
I saw an eagle flying to the east.
I came with grandma
and a dog named Honey Bun.
We went up the hill
And down the hill again.
We searched everywhere for it
and it was gone.
My grandma and I put tobacco out.

By: Brooklyn Barbra Kast,
Created 4/1/2011

I was talking to my friend Dennis on the telephone one day. I told him that I was writing books about my bird experiences and made mention of a little pretty bird that was blue. He said that he wrote a bird song for a CD then he sang it to me. He said that he was in Sedona, Arizona way high up on a hill praying and was visited by hundreds of little birds that were blue. He writes and sings Native story song's for children. My granddaughter Brooklyn had become fond of the song and liked to sing it too.

HEY LITTLE BLUE BIRD

Hey little blue bird in the sky
Why don't you come and just fly by
Hey little blue bird sitting in a tree
Why don't you come and sing a song
for me
Hey little blue bird don't you know
Singing and playing way to go
Hey little blue bird in the sky

Why don't you come and sit right by
Hey little blue bird don't you know
Come and share your spirit way to go
Hey little blue bird, hey little blue bird,
Hey little blue bird, hey little blue bird

Hey little blue bird in the sky
Why don't you come and just say hi
Hey little blue bird in the sky
Why don't you come and sit right by
In the cedar and the sage
Singing the song to pass the day

Hey little blue bird, hey little blue bird
Hey little blue bird, hey little blue bird
Hey little blue bird, hey little blue bird,
Hey little blue bird.

Dennis Dillard (White Bear)

I was walking through a land preserve around five years ago. Something moved real fast in the trees about ten to fifteen feet away from me. It was a couple of buzzards. I hadn't seen one for a long time. One flew off to a tree far away and another flew to a tree a few feet away above me. There was a bench right next to the tree below him. I sat on the bench and watched him as he watched me. I guess when one flies ahead and waits it means that it is injured or ill. They take their time and stay together as a husband and wife couple. Until they get to their destination. One usually flies ahead when they are on the lookout. They are huge birds and they were not very pretty. We hung out together for about ten to twenty minutes. I enjoyed sitting and visiting with him. I think that if I was younger I would have been horrified, screamed and ran.

One of my sisters likes to feed birds. When I was a small child she lived in a little house in the woods. The house had very large dining room windows that took up most of the walls and had a lot of bird feeders in the trees. The trees surrounded the windows. I had never seen so many different kinds of pretty birds that came to visit every morning. The trees were real close to the windows and we had a nice view of the birds. It was one of those things that a person needs to see to really appreciate. It was not the average bird watching window scenery. I remember it very well. The windows were perfectly surrounded and shaded with just right amount of sun light to see all of the birds. It was real nice to sit at the table and have breakfast being surrounded with birds in the trees. Though we were inside behind the glass it felt real good being real close to them living like we were not there but they were with us. They were real peaceful. There were very many of them and many different kinds and colors. It was a very natural feeling! If I ever have a house built, I think that something like this would be a plan.

Many times I have watched leaves fall from trees with the wind blowing and the sun shining. *They look magical and sparkling in the sun while they are floating down on to the earth. While walking my dog during one evening in the fall of 2011, I noticed that the leaves were moving on the ground to the right of me. I stopped to watch. We were standing behind my van. The leaves started to form a whirling circle on the ground and floating in a whirl, then formed into a hoop. I was amazed and thinking how exciting it would be if they came over by me and circled my dog and I. Just after that thought, the leaves in the revolving circle moved in our direction and circled us then moved to the left as a revolving circle in a line traveling west to east. They stopped a couple feet away then scattered. The feeling was amazing and it was a comforting light warm breeze. A small little whirl wind tornado of leaves had passed through our bodies. I had problems with my van earlier that day. The next day I went to my van, it started up and ran without issues. I started to think about things relating to the area around my van that had happened in the past. Then other things started to happen.*

Everything related to situations. It felt like something was tying to tell me to keep faith in regards to the future.

I had noticed the area near where I live having small whirlwinds blowing on some of the trees. The leaves swirl in circles. By looking at the hills on the ground and the way the trees grow, it is easy to see that burial mounds were built around here many years ago.

Many years ago some people used sticks as divining rods to find water and other things. The energy within the ground, trees and the paticular persons body would cause the sticks to move in the direction of the sought after things and also allow the person to know where the most energy was. There are energy lines within rows of trees and many trees drop there seeds in a lined row. This is why we see so many rows of trees. This is how many people found water in the olden days.

Many birds drop seed out of their beaks while flying. Many of the seeds that hit the soil get planted and things grow from those seeds.

Watching leaves fall off of trees can be a magical experience as well as watching the new ones grow. Where I live there are four different seasons of scenery for the many different flowers and trees. The land is constantly changing and nothing is ever the same with death, birth and rebirth. Each tree is one as we are as being ONE and all that is connected to each one is one in whole. We are one!

If we look at the earth it is one big round circular shaped ball. There is one earth and we all together on the earth with everything on the earth, as part of the one earth within the universe, and with the universe all together we are one. So if we think of one tree, it is individually one but also one within all as well as all things we are all one. We as individuals are all one with *all things within the universe. It sounds like a bit of deep thought but actually very simple.*

Things are constantly circulating within the circulation there are cycles of each living thing. Within that being life cycles and stages of birth to passing on as in, baby and childhood, young adult, midlife and elder, old, new and rebirth. The earth is constantly birthing new things.

When a seed from a tree is planted, you can see that it is down within the earth that its roots grow. The soil of the earth helps it to survive for the roots to grow. It is within the earth's soil. Trees do not belong to us and they have helped us to survive. This land does not belong to us we as well as the trees belong to the land on earth as one. I believe that the soil of the earth is holy and that we are of the earth and that every step we take on her soil beneath our feet is holy. I believe that we walk on holy ground. The earth is our mother and our home. This does not mean that we do not have our ancestral human mothers.

Females and the earth both give birth, without them there would not be men, children or anything that grows. If we do not take care of the earth everything that grows will be destroyed. The earth has a heartbeat without that heartbeat we would not be here. There has to be a balance to stay afloat and we have to stay grounded to the earth in balance. That is why we say that the drum is a heartbeat of mother earth. We all need to keep the water clean too, so that we can keep our bodies, brains, food and the earth clean. It is common sense.

It is said that the woodpecker is a drummer beating to its own drum with nature and mother earth with its own pattern and freedom. They wake people up to the truth and grounding for balance with the earth and clarity.

The woodpecker was famous within many Native American tribes for pecking holes in a branch from a tree which made a flute. They are known for bringing the flute to the many Native people. The flute has been used for many different reasons. One of the biggest purposes is to summons a loved one or for courtship. They have become very popular. Many people feel a very positive spiritual nature with playing and listening to them. They have many good spiritual purposes.

Many times I have heard people say that they need to be grounded to earth. A person as in myself as well, takes their shoes off to stand on the soil of the earth. The earth has natural minerals and vibrations that help the body to have balance. It is natural to our chemistry for balance. The earth also has a beat that is called the heartbeat of mother earth. The earth is balancing within the universe to that beat. This is why it is said that the drum beat is the beat of mother earth. The heartbeat brings balance to our natural chemistries. These things help to balance and are natural to our bodies. The soil is used by many for purification, with many different *purposes of nourishment, purification, healing and balance.*

Some people bury things in soil in the earth for purification. If you think about this, a tree has it roots in the soil. Many birds and other living things like to live in trees. Many people use mud clay dirt for healing purposes. There are minerals in soil. It also helps some types of arthritis when rubbed on the joints. It is used to stop the itch or pain and swelling of bug bites and bee stings. Many people use mud baths for this purpose, beauty treatments and spiritual purification. It works on anti-aging wrinkles by tightening and refreshing the skin. Mud clay is the number one most popular for natural beauty treatments. Some people eat little bits of mud and dirt for medicinal purposes.

Particular stones are used for purposes of healing in many different ways. Many are referred to as our grandmothers and grandfathers as they carry the spirit of our ancestors and are ancient. From around the world within most cultures, things that come from the earth's soil are holy. Some people chose to be buried in the soil when they pass on. They come from the earth then go back to the earth. Being born from the mother then going back to the mother. Some choose to be cremated or laid to rest above the earth held up by trees, depending on spiritual beliefs and as to how they want and wish for things to be. Many times stones are used on the tops of graves and for headstones. Many place flowers on the graves. They are beautiful and a sign of life for things that grow from the earth. The flowers are blessings. Stones are also known as being the bones of mother earth.

It is believed that when we go and leave that we are to go in the way of the eagle. Eagles are brave and they go in the way of the light of the sun. They are close to the creator and the earth.

The earth is our mother and alive with a heartbeat and within life all things relate. As in mining, if you poke a vein you will bleed as in digging into the soil of the earth and poking a vein. When blood hits the air it turns red then it gets darker as it dries. It becomes the colors of the earth's soil. If spilled blood does not get cleaned it can become toxic. We carry iron and minerals in our bodies and need it for survival. Our veins are dark blue. Many Native cultures have the belief that the center of the earth is dark blue. We all relate!

Many Native traditional people use trees to build their lodges which are churches. Inside the little churches we sit on the earth. Every branch and tree limb have a meaning within all of creation, lifecycles and all stages of life from every direction. Many lodges are called mother earth's womb. So we go to pray within the mother earth's womb.

These things make automatic sense to me. Think of the many different things that grow from the soil. Then think of their many different uses. We are on holy mother earth. If you think about it the earth grows grass as human grows hair. So we all have roots as well as all living things. To see an eagle flying carrying sweet grass, the eagle is carrying some of the earth's hair. Mother earths hair (grasses) holds many different used for medicines along with spiritual purposes. It is a food for many living things. Each single strand is individual with a root that holds ancestral genes that came from a seed with the ability to reproduce.

Braids can be made from hair and sweet grass. Our hair is a part of us and mother earth's hair is a part of her. Each strand is individual and has meaning as in each individual strand of a braids has meaning. These meanings have to do with natural life and cycles. We are all related within many different ways and all things relate within nature and have cycles.

Many parts of the head, mind and hair are sacred as well as the body to many cultures. There are many different types of ceremonies, anointments, blessings and baptisms that are held sacred within the cultures. Many countries with different cultures from separate parts of the world have a lot of the same cultural beliefs.

I have studied many different things wanting to know how the creator works and how people heal along with healing the earth. I have PRAYED a lot and have witnessed many MIRACLES. Not from just my prayers but in general. I have found that being close to nature and being in nature is a church of its own. To walk in nature and look around everything is holy. Nature is miraculous!

Our own beliefs make us individuals spiritually within our own reality. Our reality is our own spiritual truth. The reality may be different for others view of there own reality. Within nature we are one and have the right to be one within our own reality. Our reality may be our own cultural beliefs or no spiritual beliefs at all, meaning atheist. People from all cultures around the world can get along if they have learned this reality. According to my beliefs, discrimination is a sin!

Some cultures or persons in general refer to themselves as the human beings. In times reference to acting as human beings naturally as to another culture or person doing deliberately things that are inhumane and are considered evil. This can be with people in general as all people being part of the human race. We are the human race and we are one. We came from an individual seed that was planted and fertilized as being of the human race. Within that seed carries a mixture of our ancestors that makes an individual human being. Sometimes the word race is used for cultural, ethnicity and ancestry. In actuality we are all one race, the human race. If a person does not know their ancestral family tree or roots. It does not mean that they are not whole or one. We are all one within the universe and individual human beings.

I saw a round rainbow while at the beach one day, it was the summer of 2005. I couldn't see the bottom of it so I couldn't see if it was a complete circle. About one eighth of the circle was at the bottom close to the earth. By looking at that, it was telling me in my mind by what I saw, that the sacred hoop of life is mending. Right after that I started noticing the earth healing in different areas. A tree had bloomed that hadn't bloomed in many years. Fish were swimming in places *where fish had not lived for many years. It is a great thing to see!*

Within a mind of innocence, a child is powerful enough to retain the memory of knowing love power and the reality of it. This is why it is important to remember the innocence of children and to teach them well. I very much appreciate being taught this as a child.

I have written these stories in deep respect to all. For the people who appreciate their love of being a part of this earth our mother and the tree of life, the grandchildren, the trees that grow and sprout roots, branches and leaves of love for generations to come. In hopes of a good future for all living things as we grow on our life's path on to other generations.

About The Author

I am an Interfaith Minister, a preacher of equal rights. I am culturally mixed by heritage (Irish, Native American, English, Scottish, Spanish, French and?) My Father's Mother was Native American and most of my beliefs are Native. I believe in freedom of speech and freedom of religious rights, freedom from all forms of discrimination (race, religion, culture, disability, diversity, age and gender.) We are all one on this earth our mother and we are all created equal.

May the Creator Bless You!

Sherri Louise Jones

Co-Authors

Brooklyn
Kast
&
Dennis
Dillard

Thank you
for your
songs!

Understanding cultural

differences is

knowing that we

are all one.

THE END